DK READERS

PROFICIENT
4
READERS

SOLO SAILING

Written by Esther Ripley

DK

A Dorling Kindersley Book

The world's oceans

Two thirds of the Earth's surface is covered by its five great oceans. They are the Pacific Ocean, the Atlantic Ocean, the Indian Ocean, the Southern Ocean and the much smaller Arctic Ocean in the far, frozen North.

Solo circumnavigators

To circumnavigate the globe means to cross all 360 degrees of longitude, sailing above and below the equator. More people have climbed Mount Everest than have sailed alone around the world.

The challenge

The world's seas and oceans can be dangerous and difficult even for experienced crews to navigate.

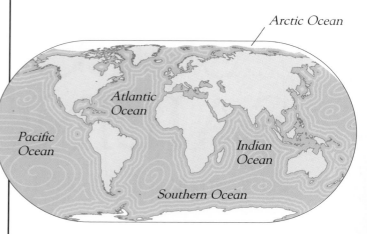

Arctic Ocean

Atlantic Ocean

Pacific Ocean

Indian Ocean

Southern Ocean

In spite of this, some adventurous sailors take on the challenge of sailing alone – overcoming the difficulties and excited by the thrills. They may face many sleepless nights riding out a storm or days of frustration sitting on a flat sea waiting for a breath of wind to catch the sails. However, in return, they may experience surfing waves at 30 knots or watching the sun rise and set with only porpoises for company.

In every sailing story in this book, there is a silent friend – the boat. Whether it's an old fishing sloop or a sleek, purpose-built yacht, both sailor and boat become the closest of friends. They look after each other through good times and bad. Of course, they sometimes fail each other, but in the end they always have an unforgettable time. ❖

Wind and sails
The diagram below shows how a sailor positions the mainsail and boom to sail with the wind, across the wind and into the wind.

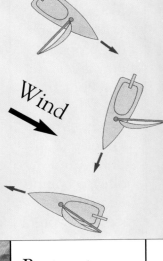

Wind

Boat parts
The bow is the front of the boat and the stern is the back. The helm is for steering and the mast and rigging (ropes and lines) support the sails.

Head

Mast

Mizzen

Mainsail

Boom

Jib

Tiller

Bowsprit

5

The first lone sailor

Joshua Slocum was a sailing shipmaster from Nova Scotia, Canada. In April 1895, he set out from Boston Harbour, Massachusetts, USA, on the first-ever solo journey around the world, in a small fishing sloop called *Spray*.

The *Spray*
In 1892, Slocum found a rotting oyster boat propped up in a field. He rebuilt this into *Spray* – a stout, strong 11-metre (37-ft) sloop with a galley, a cabin, and enough food and water storage for many months.

"Is she on course?" Slocum shouted as *Spray* bounded over the waves of the Atlantic Ocean. As he expected, there was no answer, but after days of tackling fog and gales on his own, he felt the need to test his voice. Slocum started singing the old sea shanties he used to sing as a boy, and when his voice hit the right pitch, he was joined by a school of friendly porpoises, leaping as high as the bowsprit on his boat.

Three months had passed since the 51-year-old seaman had set out on his lone voyage in his tiny sloop.

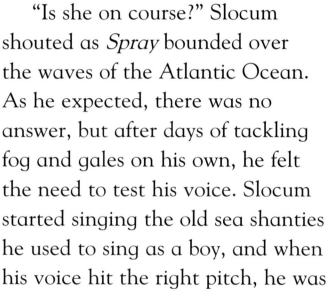

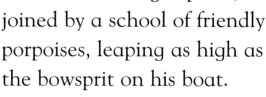

A Note to Parents and Teachers

DK READERS is a compelling reading programme for children, designed in conjunction with leading literacy experts, including Cliff Moon M.Ed., Honorary Fellow of the University of Reading. Cliff Moon has spent many years as a teacher and teacher educator specializing in reading and has written more than 140 books for children and teachers. He reviews regularly for teachers' journals.

Beautiful illustrations and superb full-colour photographs combine with engaging, easy-to-read stories to offer a fresh approach to each subject in the series. Each DK READER is guaranteed to capture a child's interest while developing his or her reading skills, general knowledge, and love of reading.

The five levels of DK READERS are aimed at different reading abilities, enabling you to choose the books that are exactly right for your child:

Pre-level 1: Learning to read
Level 1: Beginning to read
Level 2: Beginning to read alone
Level 3: Reading alone
Level 4: Proficient readers

The "normal" age at which a child begins to read can be anywhere from three to eight years old, so these levels are only a general guideline.

No matter which level you select, you can be sure that you are helping your child learn to read, then read to learn!

LONDON, NEW YORK, MUNICH,
MELBOURNE AND DEHLI

Series Editor Deborah Lock
Senior Art Editor Sonia Moore
DTP Designer Almudena Díaz
Production Alison Lenane
Picture Researcher Anna Bedewell
Picture Library Sarah Mills
Illustrator Peter Dennis
Cartographer Rob Stokes
Jacket Designer Nina Tara
Indexer Lynn Bresler
Subject Consultant Jane Russell

Reading Consultant
Cliff Moon, M.Ed.

Published in Great Britain by Dorling Kindersley Limited
80 Strand, London, WC2R 0RL

2 4 6 8 10 9 7 5 3 1

Copyright © 2005 Dorling Kindersley Limited, London

A CIP record for this book is
available from the British Library

ISBN 1-4053-03883

A Penguin Company

Colour reproduction by Colourscan, Singapore
Printed and bound in China by L Rex Printing Co., Ltd.

The publisher thanks the following for their kind permission
to reproduce their photographs:
c=centre; t=top; b=bottom; l=left; r=right
2-3: ppl/Gordon Frickers; 4-5: Alamy Images/Doug Houghton;
6: Dover Publications, Inc. New York (bl); Mary Evans Picture Library
(tl); 8: Mary Evans Picture Library (cl); 9: www.bridgeman.co.uk/ INDEX
(tr); 10: The Art Archive/Musée de la Marine Paris/Dagli Orti; 12: The
Art Archive/Biblioteca Nazionale Marciana Venice/Dagli Orti (tl);
13: Still Pictures/Mike Schroeder (tr); 14: Oxford Scientific Films/Kim
Westerkov/Photolibrary.com (tl); 15: DK Images/Science Museum (br);
Mary Evans Picture Library (tr); 17: Mary Evans Picture Library (tr);
18: Cape Ann Historical Museum (tl); Illustrated London News Picture
Library (cl); 19: Alamy Images/Popperfoto (crb); Cape Ann Historical
Museum (tr); 20: Cape Ann Historical Museum (tl); 22: Rex
Features/Chris Bott (cl); 23: Jubilee Sailing Trust (tr), (br); 24:
ppl/Chichester Archive (cl)/Robin Knox-Johnston (tl); 26: Sunday Times,
London (tl); 27: National Geographic Image Collection/Bill Curtsinger
(c); ppl/Bill Rowntree/Knox-Johnston Archive (b), (tr); 28: Sunday Times,
London (tl), (b), (br); 29: Sunday Times, London (br); Photolibrary.com (tr);
30: ppl (tl); Sunday Times, London (b); 32: Sunday Times, London (cfl);
33: ppl (br)/Bill Rowntree/Knox-Johnston Archive (t); 34: ppl (tl), (clb);
35: Corbis/David Pu'u (tr); ppl/Barry Pickthall (br); 36: ppl/ Pierre
Saboulin; 36-37: ppl/AFP (b)/Pierre Saboulin (tl); 37: ppl/Barry Pickthall
(cr); 38: Newspix Archive/Nationwide News/Chris Pavlich (tl);
38-39: ppl/RAF (b); 39: ppl (tr), (br); 40: Offshore Challenges (cfl); Rex
Features/John Downing (tl); 41: Offshore Challenges (tr); Rick Tomlinson
(c); 42: Offshore Challenges (bl), (tcl); 43: Offshore Challenges (t);
ppl/Mark Pepper (br); 44: Offshore Challenges (b); Reuters/Daniel
Joubert (tl); 45: Offshore Challenges (cr); 46-47: Rex Features;
47: Offshore Challenges (tr); Rex Features/Sipa Press (cr).
All other images © Dorling Kindersley
For further information see: www.dkimages.com

Discover more at
www.dk.com

Contents

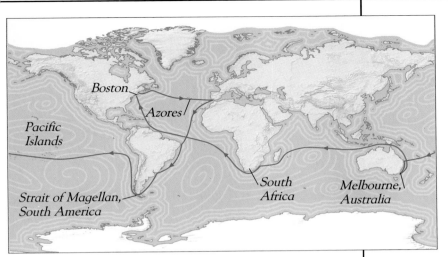

Slocum's route around the world

Labels on map: Boston, Azores, Pacific Islands, Strait of Magellan, South America, South Africa, Melbourne, Australia

When sailors on larger ships passed, they shook their heads and made the sign of the cross. They did not believe that Slocum would survive the terrible, dangerous waters of the Southern Ocean.

The route
Slocum took three years to complete his 46,000-nautical-mile round-trip. He visited South America, the Pacific Islands, Australia and South Africa.

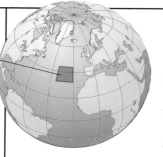

Location of the Azores

The Azores
This string of nine islands lies in the middle of the North Atlantic. They are named after a type of hawk that lives there.

Hot meals
A large iron drum with a pipe made a makeshift stove on board *Spray*. Slocum cooked Irish stew, fish chowder, fried potatoes, doughnuts and stewed pears.

In the Azores, Slocum loaded *Spray* with fresh food supplies. For supper one evening, he had a feast of plums and a special goat's cheese. By nightfall, he was doubled up with gripping pains in his stomach.

Heavy clouds were gathering and the wind was getting up. Slocum reefed in his mainsail and set his sloop on course. As he stumbled to his cabin, he knew that he had left too much sail up for the coming storm. He threw himself on the cabin floor and passed out.

As he drifted in and out of consciousness, he realised *Spray* was plunging in a heavy sea. Raising himself on one elbow, he peered out of the doorway and was amazed to see a tall man with shaggy black whiskers and a large red cap at the helm.

"Señor," said the man. "I have not come to harm you. I am one of Columbus' crew, the pilot of *Pinta*, come to help you. I will guide your ship tonight."

The *Pinta*
Pinta was one of the three ships in the fleet that brought Christopher Columbus to America in 1492. It was a caravel – a small, light and fast ship.

Rough ride
In a severe storm, sailors either 'heave to', which means to balance the jib and shortened mainsail and lash the steering to stop it from moving, or they lower all the sails and ride out the storm with bare masts.

Slocum lay on his mattress as the ghostly sailor steered *Spray* through the storm. When he woke, the decks had been washed clean and his sloop had covered 90 nautical miles dead on course throughout the night. The mystery seaman had disappeared. Whether he had been a ghost or a dream, Slocum wrote in his log: "I had the feeling that I had been in the presence of a friend."

Picking up the trade winds, *Spray* raced across the Atlantic Ocean under full sail. Delighted with his progress, Slocum spent his days reading and writing, and making meals out of the flying fish that crashed regularly onto his deck.

Trade winds
Sailing ships rely on these steady winds to blow them west across oceans. They are north-east winds above the equator and south-east winds below.

Flying fish
These unusual fish do not actively fly. They glide over the surface of the sea using their outspread pectoral fins.

He was about to head into the Strait of Magellan when a sea captain from a passing ship warned him to watch out for thieves. "You need an extra man and a dog," he said, but Slocum was determined to sail alone. So the captain handed him a packet of carpet nails.

"What do I do with these?" asked Slocum.

"Use them wisely and carefully," replied the captain, "and don't step on them yourself."

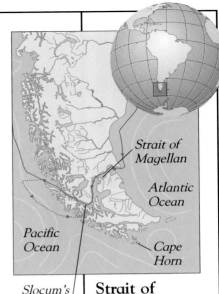

Pacific Ocean

Strait of Magellan

Atlantic Ocean

Cape Horn

Slocum's route

Strait of Magellan
This dangerous passage through the tip of South America was used by sailors to cross from the Atlantic Ocean to the Pacific Ocean. This way, they avoided the terrifying wind, waves and currents around Cape Horn. Portuguese navigator Ferdinand Magellan was the first to sail through it in 1519.

As expected, canoes swarmed
out from the shore as *Spray*
approached a quiet bay. Slocum was
alone and in great danger. When he
was sure that the bandits had seen
him, he scrambled into his cabin,
dressed in another set of clothes,
and came out at the other end.
"Now they think there are two of
us," he thought. Then he dressed
a piece of bowsprit in clothes and
attached a rope so he could make
it move. This made three sailors.

As the first canoe came closer, Slocum shouted orders to his pretend crew and fired his gun. The canoes turned back for the shore, but he guessed they would return.

The ferocious winds around the tip of South America, called Williwaws, forced *Spray* backwards rather than forwards to the Pacific Ocean. During the night, Slocum stayed grimly at the helm with fierce squalls of hail and sleet cutting into his skin.

Fierce winds
Williwaws are screaming winds that race down the mountains and whip up freak waves around Cape Horn. Squalls are sudden bursts of wind with rain or sleet.

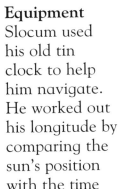

Equipment
Slocum used his old tin clock to help him navigate. He worked out his longitude by comparing the sun's position with the time on his clock.

13

White water
When the sea churns with white spray, it means danger – a reef or rock lies just below the surface.

Charts
These maps of the sea and shore give vital details about water depth, currents and underwater hazards, such as reefs and rocks.

When day broke, Slocum realised he had been heading into the dangerous waters called the Milky Way, where white water foams around sunken rocks. It was a miracle that *Spray* had not been smashed to pieces.

Picking a channel through the rocks, Slocum reached calm water and put down anchor in a small cove. Just before he went to bed, he remembered to take out his packet of nails and sprinkle them over the deck.

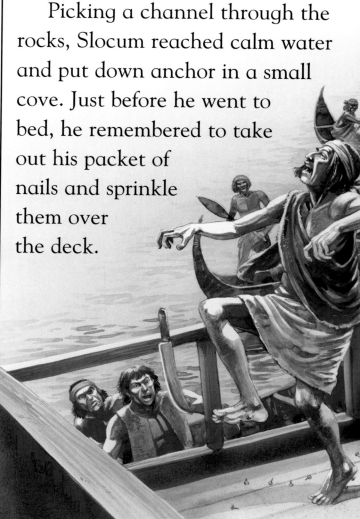

In the middle of the night, Slocum was woken up by the sound of howling and shrieking. Barefooted thieves had crept on board and were now plunging off the side of the boat with sharp nails in their feet. Slocum scared them off with a volley of shots.

Navigating
A navigator works out a ship's position (latitude) using an instrument to measure the height of the sun at noon, or the position of the stars.

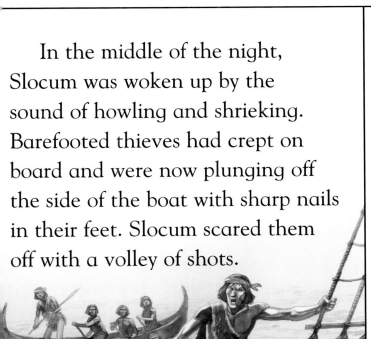

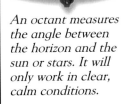

An octant measures the angle between the horizon and the sun or stars. It will only work in clear, calm conditions.

15

People read about Slocum's voyage in newspaper reports. He was entertained by naval officers, leaders, and even royalty in many of the ports he visited.

Unwanted gifts
In the West Indies, Slocum was given a goat that became an onboard eating machine, destroying his charts, a sail and his straw hat. He unloaded it at the next port.

Slocum had been sailing for more than a year when he headed out into the vast stretches of the South Pacific. He now needed to raise funds to continue his journey. In the Pacific Islands, he cooked doughnuts on *Spray* and sold them to the islanders. They paid him with gold coins that they had rescued from a sunken galleon. In Melbourne, Australia, he charged visitors money to look at a large shark he had caught.

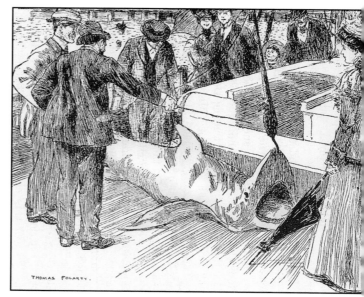

The 3.8-metre (12-ft, 6-in) shark was laid out on the deck of Spray *for the visitors to see.*

In South Africa, Slocum was treated as an honoured guest and introduced to President Kruger of the Transvaal region as "the man who is on a voyage around the world". There was a long silence.

"You don't mean around the world," roared the president. "It is impossible. You mean *in* the world." Slocum realised that President Kruger and his followers still believed that the world was flat!

On 25 June, 1898, Slocum was within days of home when a tornado swept along the northeast coast of America, bringing down buildings and trees. Although *Spray* was badly battered, Slocum sailed into Boston and on to Fairhaven – the place where he first restored the old sloop. "I could bring her no nearer home," he said. His extraordinary journey had taken three years. ❖

Transvaal flat worlders
Before the first explorers found that it was possible to sail around the world, many people believed that the Earth was a flat disc.

Afterwards . . .
After his return, Slocum wrote a book about his voyage called *Sailing Alone Around the World.* He continued to sail *Spray* and at the age of 65 set out on a solo voyage to South America. He was never seen again.

The sailor with no fingers

Howard Blackburn sailed alone across the Atlantic from Gloucester, Massachusetts, USA, to Gloucester, England, in his fishing sloop, *Great Western*, in 1899. His achievement was all the more amazing because of the physical disability he had to overcome.

The first across
In 1876, Alfred Centennial Johnson was the first to cross the Atlantic Ocean alone. He did it for a dare.

The *Great Western*
The 9-metre (30-ft) sloop was purpose-built for the journey across the Atlantic.

"The *Great Western's* here – he made it after all!"

As the shout went up, the crowd on England's Gloucester docks surged forward as *Great Western* was towed up the canal and moored. Everyone was very eager to get a glimpse of Howard Blackburn, the stranger who had sailed unaided across the Atlantic Ocean. There was a gasp as the tall, sunburnt American reached out to shake hands with the Deputy Mayor – the sailor had no fingers and only half a thumb on each of his hands.

As a young man, Blackburn had worked on a fishing schooner on the bitterly cold fishing banks off Newfoundland.

He was laying out trawl nets from a smaller fishing boat with his mate when a storm blew up and they lost sight of the schooner. By morning, the ship had gone and their only chance of survival was to row the 60 nautical miles to the coast. Blackburn gripped the oars until his hands froze around them like claws and rowed for four days until he reached a settlement at a river mouth. Huddled in the stern of the boat, his poor mate had frozen to death. The settlers nursed Blackburn back to health, but his frostbitten fingers and toes could not be saved.

Fishing
Fishermen laid out trawl lines with baited hooks to catch halibut.
On a good trip, they returned to port laden with fish.

Frostbite
Frostbitten fingers become swollen, grey and numb, and, in severe cases, they fall off.

19

Saloon owner
Blackburn was no longer able to fish, so he opened a saloon on the waterfront. It was always crowded with fishermen who never tired of hearing his terrible tale.

Hand tricks
Instead of using a hook on each hand to replace his fingers, Blackburn taught himself tricks. He held a pen with his stubby thumbs and developed so much strength he could pick up pennies in the crease of his palm.

After what had happened to Blackburn, it is hard to imagine how he could ever go to sea again, but the attraction of the ocean is strong. Sixteen years later, he designed and built a small Gloucester sloop boat, 9 metres (30 ft) long with extra short and long lines attached to the sails to make it easier for him to control them.

To raise the sails, he ran the rope, or halyard, around his waist and leaned back until the rope was tight. Then he used his thumbs to pin down the rope while he hauled the slack around a hook, or cleat, with his teeth.

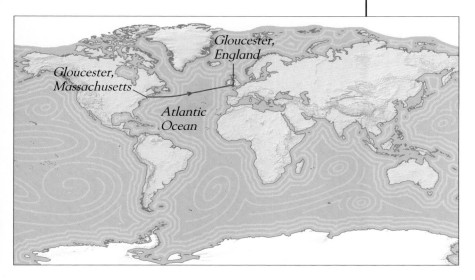

Blackburn's route from Gloucester, Massachusetts, USA, to Gloucester, England

Blackburn's terrible fishing story had made him famous, and 10,000 people lined Gloucester harbour in Massachusetts to wish him well on his voyage across the Atlantic Ocean. He took enough food provisions to last five men at least 90 days.

"I might meet someone on the way who needs some," he said. Blackburn had not forgotten the struggle for survival during his four days in a freezing fishing boat without food or water.

Gloucester, Massachusetts
By the end of the 19th century, Gloucester was the world's busiest fishing port. In the 1920s, it became famous as the place where Clarence Birdseye first managed to freeze, package and sell frozen food.

A tough start

To begin with, Blackburn was sailing in dense fog, and the cold clammy air was seeping into his bones. For eight days, he was feverish and one foot became very swollen.

Atlantic record

In January 2003, 15-year-old Seb Clover became the youngest to cross the Atlantic Ocean single-handed. He was racing his father. They took 21 days – his Dad won.

Blackburn sailed just south of the transatlantic steamer route. As he rustled up a meal in his galley one night, a blast from a whistle sent him racing on deck. The huge bulk of a steamer twice as high as his mast loomed above him. It had spotted his two white lights and shuddered to a halt – just in time.

The west winds carried *Great Western* halfway to England, but then the wind died and the water became calm. When Blackburn finally picked up an east wind, he stayed awake for 38 hours to make up for lost time. Day after day he tacked through heavy seas, screeching wind and pelting rain. Then he woke one morning to see the coast of England shimmering in the bright August sunshine. After 62 days at sea, Blackburn docked at Gloucester and was called a hero once again. ❖

Sailing for the disabled

The spirit of sailors like Blackburn lives on in sailing charities that give young people with disabilities the chance to go sailing. *Tenacious* is a tall ship with special equipment that allows disabled young people to crew alongside able-bodied sailors.

Hoisted up the mast of Tenacious *by ropes and pulleys.*

The first race around the world

The Golden Globe was the first-ever single-handed, non-stop sailing race around the world. It was organised by the English newspaper *The Sunday Times* in 1968. Robin Knox-Johnston, Bernard Moitessier and Donald Crowhurst were three of the nine competitors.

The prize
The globe on the top of the Golden Globe trophy showed the route around the world.

Sir Francis
The Queen knighted Chichester for achieving the first one-stop solo circum-navigation in his yacht, *Gypsy Moth IV*.

In 1967, Francis Chichester sailed around the world and put into port just once for repairs in Australia. His story was so inspiring that the following year a newspaper organised a non-stop sailing race around the world.

The first sailor home would win the Golden Globe trophy, and the finisher with the fastest time would win a prize of £5,000 (about $12,000). Each sailor could depart at any time between June 1 and October 31 as long as he started and finished at the same port.

In many ways, this challenging race was a foolhardy adventure.

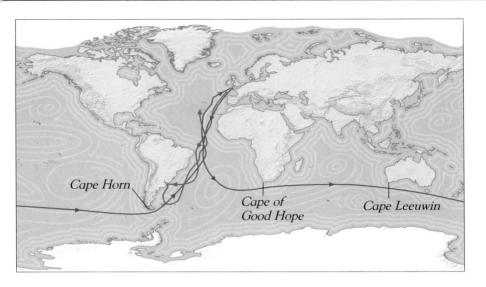

Cape Horn

Cape of
Good Hope

Cape Leeuwin

The route: Key points along the route were the Cape of Good Hope on the tip of Africa, Cape Leeuwin on the tip of Australia and Cape Horn on the tip of South America.

● *Red route: The route plotted for the Golden Globe competitors to circumnavigate the world*

● *Green route: The ill-fated route of Donald Crowhurst, one of the competitors*

The route took the competitors into the treacherous waters that surrounded Antarctica. Here storms roared up out of nowhere, shredding sails, cracking masts and capsizing yachts. Radio contact was difficult. If disaster struck, there was almost no hope of rescue.

This is what happened to three of the competitors who took up the challenge.

Starting points
The nine competitors had to start from England. Knox-Johnston set off from Falmouth in Cornwall on June 14; Moitessier started from Plymouth in Devon on August 22; and Crowhurst, who was the last to leave, left from Teignmouth in Devon just a few hours before the deadline on October 31.

25

Robin
Knox-Johnston was a merchant marine captain. He was sailing in a 9.7-metre (32-ft) long ketch called *Suhaili,* which had been built in India.

Daily swim
Knox-Johnston liked to swim from his yacht, something most sailors are too nervous to do. He trailed a line from the boat, swam alongside, and pulled himself back on board.

Robin Knox-Johnston was comfortable on board his yacht, *Suhaili,* but within weeks it became clear that the boat had a major leak.

Pulling on a snorkel and mask, Knox-Johnston jumped into the sea to take a look. He found gaping cracks between the planks on both sides of the hull. The only solution was caulking – jamming material in the cracks and waterproofing it. This was hard enough to do underwater, but in these warm seas off West Africa, Knox-Johnston would be mending his boat surrounded by sharks.

As he prepared his tools, Knox-Johnston watched a shark circling the boat. He fetched his rifle and threw paper onto the water, and as the shark reared its head to bite, he fired. He suspected that two more sharks lurked below the boat.

But the wind was getting up and he needed to repair his boat before the weather changed. He slipped quietly into the water and began to fill the cracks. Four hours passed. Miraculously, the sharks ignored him – and the leaks were fixed.

Suhaili
Knox-Johnston had already sailed his heavy teak yacht 10,000 nautical miles from India and was used to living on board.

Sharks lurking in the shadows under a boat.

Supplies
The yacht was loaded with 1,500 assorted cans of corned beef, sausages, steak, baked vegetables and beans, condensed milk and processed cheese.

27

Bernard Moitessier was now four months into the race. He was steering his steel ketch, *Joshua*, around a dangerous reef off Stewart Island, to the south of New Zealand. During the afternoon, dark clouds gathered overhead, hiding the island from view.

Sailing light
Moitessier was a French sailor and writer. He managed to sail fast by keeping his metal boat as light as possible. He threw all his non-essential supplies overboard.

Stewart Island
The reefs off Stewart Island in New Zealand are know as the South Trap because of the many ships that have foundered on them.

Suddenly a large school of porpoises appeared around the boat and began some puzzling behaviour. A large group of them formed lines along the starboard (right) side of the boat and began rushing from stern (back) to bow (front) and then veering sharply to the right. They repeated this over and over again.

After watching for a while, Moitessier checked his location and was horrified to find that the wind had shifted and he was heading north – straight for the reef. As he altered course to the east, his boat swung sharply to the right. The porpoises' message now made perfect sense.

Now that the yacht was out of danger, the porpoises swam playfully around the boat. They stayed with Moitessier until he had safely passed the reef.

Porpoises enjoy riding in the bow waves of boats.

Making contact
Moitessier refused to take a radio. He used a slingshot to send messages to his family and film to his sponsors. He hurled the packages onto the decks of passing boats.

Inexperienced
Crowhurst, an electronics engineer designed his own trimaran – a yacht with three parallel hulls – but he had never sailed one before.

Donald Crowhurst was uneasy about the voyage ahead as he sailed *Teignmouth Electron* out into a grey mist off the coast of Devon, England. He had designed a unique computer-operated system that would adjust his sails, report conditions and trigger a buoyancy bag if his boat capsized. All the wires were in place, but inside the cabin they ended in a tangle, as he'd had no time to install the computer.

TEIGNMOUTH EL

Back on the quay in Teignmouth, Devon, he had also left behind some essential tools and spare wood for repairs.

Crowhurst made very slow progress, and out in the Atlantic Ocean his problems increased. The hatches were leaking, soaking his generator with seawater and leaving him without electricity. The hulls leaked too, and he had to bail out water with a bucket. But instead of abandoning the race, Crowhurst began to cheat. He radioed a report saying that he was sailing at record-breaking speeds and gave a position that was way ahead of his actual location. He also started a new logbook – from now on he planned to fake all the details of his journey.

Unlucky boat
When *Teignmouth Electron* was launched, the champagne bottle did not smash on her hull. Sailors believe this is a sign of bad luck.

Logbook
Sailors keep a daily record of their course, speed, progress and weather conditions in a logbook. Race officials study the books at the end of a race.

31

Moitessier liked to meditate on deck, enjoying the solitude of his lone voyage. After he abandoned the race, he sailed halfway around the world again to Tahiti.

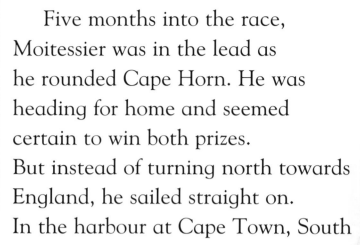

The finish
Robin Knox-Johnston was the only man to return to the port he started from. Everyone else abandoned the race or had to be rescued from their stricken yachts.

Five months into the race, Moitessier was in the lead as he rounded Cape Horn. He was heading for home and seemed certain to win both prizes.
But instead of turning north towards England, he sailed straight on.
In the harbour at Cape Town, South Africa, he tossed a package with a message to a passing ship. "I am happy at sea," the message read, "so I am sailing on." He hated to think of all the attention he would get as the winner of the race.
When Knox-Johnston arrived back in Falmouth to win the Golden Globe, parts of his boat were held together by pieces of string. The storms around the Cape of Good Hope had almost torn *Suhaili* apart. But whenever Knox-Johnston had been on the point of giving up, he had made a repair and kept going.

The winner, Knox-Johnston, arrives back in Falmouth Harbour after 312 days at sea.

Only Crowhurst was left in the race now. While everyone believed he was sailing around the world, he had actually spent months zigzagging slowly in the Atlantic Ocean. But the terrible lie was more than he could bear. He stopped all radio reports. Two weeks later, a Royal Mail ship spotted *Teignmouth Electron* drifting aimlessly. Crowhurst was not on board – and he was never found. ❖

Drifting
Inside Crowhurst's cabin, dirty dishes were piled in the sink and electrical parts were scattered everywhere. A life raft was still on board.

Amazing rescues

In 1996-1997, an English businessman named **Tony Bullimore** (left) and Frenchman **Thierry Dubois** (right) were competing in the Vendée Globe – a single-handed, non-stop, round-the-world race. They both met with unexpected disaster in the Southern Ocean.

Exide Challenger
Bullimore's yacht cost £500,000 to build and had an extra long keel to keep it upright.

The route
The two men sailed down the Atlantic and were heading east to Australia when the storm hit. Dubois had made one stop for repairs.

December 31st

Tony Bullimore's ketch-rigged yacht, *Exide Challenger*, glided sweetly over the waves in a gentle breeze. He ate breakfast, hung out his laundry and shaved. He was 1,400 nautical miles southwest of Perth, Australia, deep in the Southern Ocean, and he had not been expecting this kind of weather.

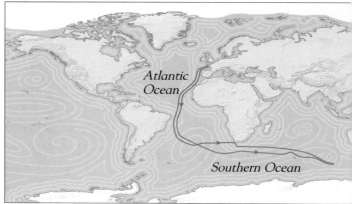

Atlantic Ocean

Southern Ocean

Bullimore and Dubois capsized in the Southern Ocean.

January 4th   Conditions changed fast. A huge storm was building, so Bullimore reduced his sails. Ahead, he could see a wave as tall as an eight-storey building.

Clipping on his safety harness, Bullimore surfed down the swells as huge waves reared on all sides of his boat. He took down all his sails and was in his cabin making tea when there was a sickening crack above him. The mast had broken – *Exide Challenger* rolled over, and its keel broke off and was swept away. As freezing water flooded the cabin, Bullimore set off the distress signal on his beacon.

Freak waves in the Southern Ocean can be three times as high as the one in this picture.

Help signals
A distress signal from an Argos beacon or EPIRB (Emergency Position Indicating Radio Beacon) is picked up by satellites orbiting the Earth and relayed to rescue stations. Rescuers can pinpoint a signal to within 300 metres (984 ft).

The same storm had hit **Thierry Dubois** in his yacht, *Pour Amnesty International,* just 10 nautical miles away. A deep, roaring wave smashed the hull upside down and broke the mast in three places. The boat quickly righted itself but then capsized three more times – and stayed upside down. Dubois set off his beacon, put on his survival suit and struggled out of the escape hatch. Lashed by bitterly cold spray and wind, he tried to launch his life raft, but a wave snatched it away.

Pour Amnesty International
The yacht was named after the charity Amnesty International. Dubois was raising awareness of their campaign to improve life for disadvantaged children all over the world.

All he could do now was hold on to the rudder of his upturned yacht and wait.

January 6th An Australian airforce search-and-rescue plane flew low over the towering waves. The pilot spotted the tiny figure of Dubois perched on the hull and dropped a life raft. Dubois plunged into the icy waves and threw himself onto it, but it flipped over and was swept away. To his horror, Dubois found he could no longer reach his yacht or the life raft. The wind was making it difficult for the pilot to drop more rafts, but finally he hit the target. By the time Dubois hauled himself inside the raft, he had been in the sea for half an hour.

Survival suits
These insulated, waterproof suits keep the wearer afloat and protected from the cold for up to six hours in freezing water.

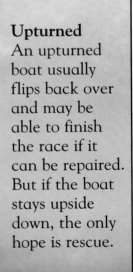

Upturned
An upturned boat usually flips back over and may be able to finish the race if it can be repaired. But if the boat stays upside down, the only hope is rescue.

Adelaide, an Australian frigate, set out from Perth, Australia, carrying Seahawk helicopters for the rescue. It made slow progress in the storm.

For two days and three nights, Dubois sat huddled in the life raft eating his emergency supplies and reading a survival manual. At last, he heard the whir of helicopter blades overhead. A voice called out "You want a lift, guy?"

Within minutes, the Frenchman was winched to safety.

Frigates and Seahawks
These Navy warships are also used for rescue. The Seahawk pilots can land on flight decks that roll and pitch in heavy sea and fly low over the waves looking for survivors.

Life rafts
Once a survivor is in the raft, he is fully enclosed and protected. Food, water and blankets are on board, as well as a hand-held radio so he can be in touch with the rescue operation.

Later the same day, the frigate reached *Exide Challenger*. The yacht was still floating upside down, but there was no sign of life. A boat was launched and one of the crew tapped on the hull of the yacht. A deep "hello!" came from inside. Then, Bullimore swam out.

"I thought it was time to put in an appearance," he said.

He had spent the last five days in his survival suit stretched out on a narrow shelf in semi-darkness. The water level was creeping up inside the cabin. "Soon I would be bobbing about like a ping-pong ball in a washing machine," he said.

When he was safely on board the *Adelaide*, the first thing he asked for was a cup of tea. ❖

Tony Bullimore emerging from the upturned Exide Challenger.

Warm wrap
Bullimore was wrapped in an aluminium-backed "space blanket" to keep him warm. He was suffering from cold and dehydration, but had managed to survive on a few pieces of chocolate and a little water.

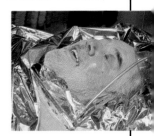

Sailing a dream

Englishwoman **Ellen MacArthur** was just 24 years old when she was given a chance to compete in the 2000-2001 Vendée Globe single-handed, non-stop, round-the-world race – and make an important impact on the solo-sailing world.

Repairs at sea
All solo sailors have to be able to repair their boats, including complicated electronic gear.

Christmas
After nearly two months at sea, MacArthur opened the gifts her family had stowed on board and put up a tinsel tree.

It was Christmas Eve, but Ellen MacArthur had more to think about than putting a star on top of her Christmas tree. She was climbing the 28-metre (90-ft) mast of her yacht, *Kingfisher*. The day before, a sail had been torn away by the wind, breaking the halyard – the rope that raises and lowers the sail. If MacArthur was to carry on in the race, she had to drag 183 metres (200 ft) of heavy rope and a tool kit to the top of the mast.

Kingfisher pitched and tossed in the swell. One careless move and she would either crash onto the deck or plunge into the freezing sea.

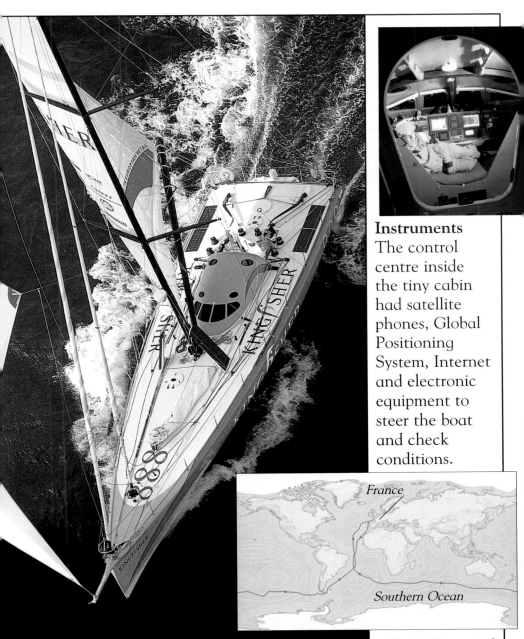

Instruments
The control centre inside the tiny cabin had satellite phones, Global Positioning System, Internet and electronic equipment to steer the boat and check conditions.

France

Southern Ocean

MacArthur was shaking with cold as she connected the new halyard and began the long journey back down.

The 23,000-nautical-mile race starts and finishes at Les Sables d'Olonne in the Vendée region of France. It circles the globe in the Southern Ocean.

Water baby

Ellen loved everything to do with the sea. Aged five, she took a trip on her aunt's yacht and decided that it was the best thing in the world.

Influences

Ellen's favourite books were by Sir Francis Chichester and Sir Robin Knox-Johnston. She loved to pretend to sail by chalking out islands and harbours in the playground.

Iduna *moored in a bay in Scotland during Ellen's around Britain trip.*

Although MacArthur grew up on a small farm in Derbyshire, England, a long way from the sea, she had always wanted to sail. She saved every penny of her pocket money to buy her first dinghy and then saved all her school lunch money to buy a bigger boat. When there was no room left in her bedroom for her yachting equipment, she moved her bed out into the barn.

But sailing for fun on rivers and estuaries is quite different from sailing single-handed on the open ocean. In her school library, MacArthur read books by the world's greatest lone sailors over and over again. When she bought her third boat, a sturdy sea-worthy Corribee 21 called *Iduna*, she stripped out the cabin and left just one bunk.

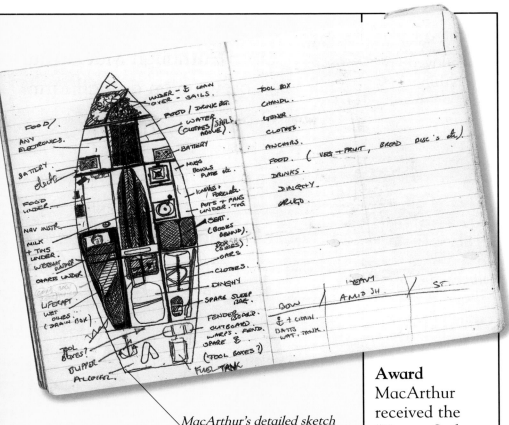

MacArthur's detailed sketch of the plan for Iduna.

Maybe that's when she decided she would be going solo, too.

At age 18, MacArthur became "Young Sailor of the Year". After making her first solo voyage around Britain, she spent the next six years teaching sailing, learning to mend and maintain a boat, and racing in chartered yachts before she found a sponsor for the Vendée Globe race.

Award
MacArthur received the "Young Sailor of the Year" award in recognition of her outstanding results for a Royal Yachting Association certificate.

At the start of the Vendée Globe, 24 yachts jostled for position in a blustery gale as they set off from the west coast of France. MacArthur's nerves settled and she began to enjoy life on her sparkling new boat. She was in control of a beautiful, sleek, purpose-built yacht. "*Kingfisher* is an amazing friend," she wrote in her log.

They're off
The *Kingfisher* team stayed on board until the yacht reached the start zone. When the gun was fired, the competitors were on their own – each one battling to get ahead.

Doldrums
Yachts can be trapped for days or even weeks in the Doldrums. This area of flat sea with no wind lies close to the equator and separates the north and south trade winds.

On day two of the race, MacArthur was in third place – she had made a great start. But as *Kingfisher* entered the Doldrums, everything changed. The sails hung flat, the sun beat down on the deck, and the tiny cabin heated up like a greenhouse. MacArthur used the time well to repair the mainsail. As soon as she rehoisted the sail, the wind picked up.

"Now we are ready to sail south and *Kingfisher* seems pleased," she wrote. At midnight, MacArthur was working in shorts and a T-shirt, the moon shining brightly above her. She followed the sailor's custom of offering a gift to Neptune, the Roman god of the sea, by pouring champagne into the ocean as she crossed the equator.

This engraving shows Neptune in his shell chariot.

Night sailing
MacArthur never slept for more than 5 hours and often for only 20 minutes at a time. She dozed in the long seat in front of her instruments until a sudden change in the weather or the yacht triggered an alarm that woke her up.

A wrist monitor recorded how much she slept.

Ready meals
To make hot meals, MacArthur added boiling water to packets of freeze-dried food.

Icebergs
These floating blocks of ice and snow are even more dangerous than they look because most of their vast bulk lies below the waterline. Sailors also have to watch out for growlers – ice chunks as big as a car that can sink a boat when they collide.

As *Kingfisher* neared Cape Horn, the winds pushed her off course. The boat headed south into ice fields, and MacArthur felt helpless. She screamed, "Why us? Please give us a chance!"

Carefully, MacArthur guided *Kingfisher* past walls of ice and glittering blue caves.

Back on course, MacArthur was catching up the race leader when one of the forestays that held up the mast snapped. Despite the danger that the mast would break under the strain of a big sail, MacArthur unfurled the gennaker and let *Kingfisher* spring to life.

As she neared the French coast, MacArthur could hear fireworks – Michel Desjoyeaux had crossed the finishing line. But when she stepped from *Kingfisher* into a blaze of camera lights and cheering crowds, she was a winner too. She was the youngest Briton and the fastest female sailor to sail solo non-stop around the world.

However, many people say that records are made to be broken. Who knows who will be the youngest or the fastest solo sailor in the future? ❖

***Kingfisher* team** MacArthur was given a huge welcome home from her team. She was just one day and 250 nautical miles behind the winner.

The winner The Frenchman Desjoyeaux set a new Vendée Globe record with his yacht *PRB*. He finished the race in 93 days and claimed the £80,000 prize.

Glossary

Beacon
Sailors keep one type of beacon on board the boat and some wear a personal beacon, so they can be found if the boat sinks or they are washed overboard.

Boom
A free-swinging spar (pole) attached to the mast at one end that supports the bottom of a sail.

Forestay
A line that runs from the bow (front) to the top of the mast to help support the mast.

Galleon
A large sailing ship with three or four masts, used for trade and fighting from the 15th to the 18th centuries. Many galleons were sunk or shipwrecked with precious stones and gold on board.

Galley
The kitchen area of a boat.

Gennaker
A large balloon-like sail set on the front of the boat.

Global Postioning System
A navigation system that uses satellites orbiting the Earth to pinpoint the exact position of a boat to within a few metres (feet).

Hatch
An opening on the deck into the inside of a boat.

Hull
The main body of a boat.

Jib
A triangular sail at the very front of a boat.

Ketch
A yacht with two masts.

Knot
A measure for speed at sea. A boat that is sailing at one nautical mile per hour is travelling at a speed of one knot.

Latitudes
Imaginary horizontal lines around the earth that are measured in degrees north or south of the equator (0° latitude).

Longitude
Imaginary vertical lines from the North to the South Pole that divide the earth into segments measured from 0 to 180 degrees east or west of the vertical line through Greenwich, England.

Mainsail
The biggest sail attached to the back of the mainmast.

Nautical mile
This measurement is one eighth longer than a land mile.

Reefing
Reducing the area of any sail in strong winds.

Rudder
A plate or board mounted vertically beneath the stern (back) of a boat that can be turned to the left or right to steer the boat.

Satellite phones
Telephones that can send and receive signals from anywhere on Earth using satellites orbiting the Earth.

Schooner
A sailing ship with at least two masts, the aft (back) mast being at least as tall as the foremast.

Sloop
A yacht with one mast.

Steamer
A large ocean-going ship powered by steam engines.

Tall ship
Old-style sailing boats and ships with traditional rigging used mostly for training and historical research.

Transvaal
The Transvaal Republic was established by Afrikaaner settlers and taken over by the British in 1902. It is now part of South Africa.